IMAGES
of America

ROUTE 66 IN ST. LOUIS

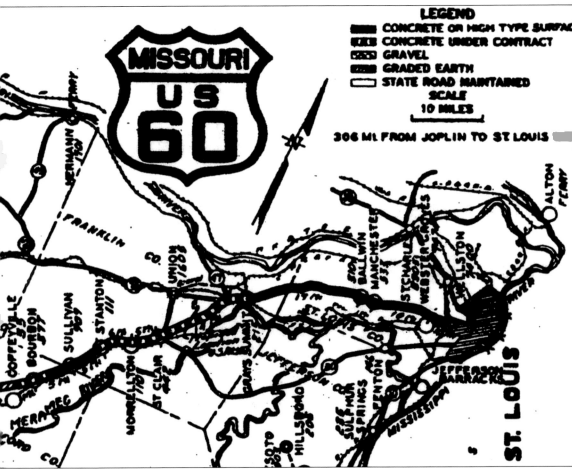

This 1926 Missouri map shows how planners originally envisioned the highway between Chicago and Los Angeles with the number 60. But the governor of Kentucky demanded that the more-important-sounding 60 go through his state. Angry telegrams flew. In August 1926, Missouri and Oklahoma officials agreed to compromise and use 66.

On the cover: The Chain of Rocks Bridge opened on July 20, 1929, and was originally painted silver. The Corps of Engineers ordered that the main span must face the water flow directly over the main channel. So the 24-degree bend was necessary to bring the bridge ashore on land the promoters owned on the Missouri side. (Courtesy of the Missouri Historical Society.)

IMAGES
of America

ROUTE 66 IN ST. LOUIS

Joe Sonderman

ARCADIA
PUBLISHING

Published by Arcadia Publishing
Charleston, South Carolina

Printed in the United States of America

Library of Congress Catalog Card Number: 2007941896

For all general information contact Arcadia Publishing at:
Telephone 843-853-2070
Fax 843-853-0044
E-mail sales@arcadiapublishing.com
For customer service and orders:
Toll-Free 1-888-313-2665

Visit us on the Internet at www.arcadiapublishing.com

For Lorraine, Cathy, Kim, and roadies everywhere

CONTENTS

ACKNOWLEDGMENTS

Thank you to Anna Wilson and John Pearson at Arcadia Publishing. Laura Jolley at the Missouri State Archives helped find some great shots. Thanks to Patsy Starks at the St. Clair History Museum and to Mary Westerhold and Marion Sperling at the Madison County Historical Society. No book on Route 66 in St. Louis would be possible without the exhaustive research of Jim Powell, founder of the Missouri Route 66 Association, and the late Skip Curtis, author of *The Missouri U.S. 66 Tour Book*. Unless otherwise indicated, all images are from the author's collection.

INTRODUCTION

The first road west from St. Louis was an extension of Market Street called Rue Bonhomme, after Joseph Hebert. He was a good man, or *bonhomme* in French. The Missouri General Assembly established the first state road in 1835. It led to the quiet village of Manchester and then to Jefferson City. The road between St. Louis and St. James saw traffic increase about the time Missouri joined the union, when iron ore was discovered in the Meramec Valley. On February 6, 1837, the State of Missouri authorized a state road between St. Louis and Springfield. The route became known as the Springfield Road.

Route 66 west from St. Louis combined several older routes. Gravois took its name from the French for *gravelly*. Chippewa is an Ojibway name for the puckered seams on a type of moccasins. On February 5, 1845, a group of St. Louis County residents led by Wesley Watson filed a petition for a road "from Cooper's Farm on the Old Manchester Roads, thence to the River Des Peres near the mouth of the Lick Branch, from thence the most practical route to a ferry landing opposite the town of Fenton."

Watson's Road connected with the Antire Road at Meramec Station (Valley Park). Antire Road ran west from the Dougherty Mill and Ferry to the property of "widow Votaw" west of the Meramec River (Times Beach). The Blakey Road ran from the widow Votaw's place to Eureka. Originally laid out as the Franklin Road in 1856, the Eureka-Allenton Road was officially accepted on April 21, 1862. In the 1840s, the government established a stage line between St. Louis and Springfield. Telegraph lines gave it the name Wire Road. The Blue and the Gray marched along the dusty trail on their way to fight and die at Carthage and Wilson's Creek. Bushwhackers and guerillas used it to spread terror in the Ozark countryside. After the war, the government took down the wires and left the lonely poles.

The railways dominated travel after the Civil War, and the rutted country lanes were maintained mainly to provide access to the railway. Bicycle enthusiasts were the first to push for good roads. The first cars came to the state in 1891. In 1907, the state appointed a highway engineer under the board of agriculture to help counties with construction of roads that would someday be part of a state system. Meanwhile, promoters were weaving a tangled web. They gave their road an important-sounding name and painted color-coded stripes on fence posts, telegraph poles, or any handy surface. Drivers followed the colors to travel the Lincoln Highway, the Dixie Highway, or the Old Spanish Trail. In 1917, an association mapped out the Ozark Trail from St. Louis to Romeroville, New Mexico. From there, it joined the National Old Trails Road to Los Angeles. The associations made money from "contributions" by merchants to have the highway routed past their businesses. Drivers were often taken miles out of their way. Missouri voters took action in 1920, approving a $60 million road bond issue for a state road system to "Lift Missouri Out of the Mud." In August 1922, the state highway commission designated routes connecting the big cities. The road between St. Louis and Joplin was designated as State Highway 14.

The American Association of State Highway and Transportation Officials, or AASHTO, assigned even numbers to east–west highways in November 1925. North–south routes were given odd numbers. The most important east–west routes ended in zero, and the principal north–south routes would end in one or five. The proposed Route 60 was an exception. The important-sounding number was not assigned to a completely transcontinental route. It was assigned to the highway between Chicago and Los Angeles.

Maps were already printed up in Missouri showing Route 60. But Gov. William J. Fields of Kentucky wanted 60 for the highway running between Newport News to a point near Springfield. The highway between Chicago and Los Angeles was to be designated 62. That did not fly with Missouri State Highway Commission chief engineer A. H. Piepmeier and Cyrus Avery, chairman of the Oklahoma Department of Highways. They insisted on 60 for the Chicago to Los Angeles route.

The battle continued until April 1926, when Avery noted that the catchy-sounding 66 was still unclaimed. On April 30, 1926, Avery and Piepmeier agreed to accept 66. The final routes and numbers of the Federal Highway System were approved on November 11, 1926.

The Route 66 boosters went to work. Billboards went up, maps went out, and press releases flowed. It was foot power that really put Route 66 on the map. C. C. "Cash and Carry" Pyle promoted a footrace from Los Angeles to Chicago along 66 before swinging toward the finish line—in New York City. On March 4, 1928, some 275 runners started the Bunion Derby. Just 55 remained when a part-Cherokee runner from the Route 66 town of Foyil, Oklahoma, crossed the finish line on May 26. Andy Payne won $25,000, Pyle lost a pile of money, and Route 66 reaped the publicity.

C. H. Laessig had opened the first gas station in the United States on Theresa Street in St. Louis in 1905. Early motorists avoided the fancy big-city hotels. At first, they just camped beside the road. But farmers soon had their fill of the "tin can tourists." Some communities, eager for travelers' business, started up free campgrounds. There was one in Forest Park. But the camps began attracting undesirables, and the city closed the camp in 1928. By then, motels were springing up along the highway west of St. Louis.

Songwriter Bobby Troup said on a trip west, his wife, Cynthia, suggested he pen a song about Route 40. Troup said that would be silly, since they would soon be on Route 66. Just outside St. Louis, his wife whispered, "Get your kicks on Route 66." First released in 1946 by Nat King Cole, the song has since been recorded by dozens of artists as diverse as the Rolling Stones and Depeche Mode.

Even during the postwar golden age, change was in the air. Dwight David Eisenhower had seen how Germany's autobahns were vital to the military. Eisenhower also saw building roads as a way to stimulate the economy. Congress passed his Federal Highway Aid Act in 1956, creating the interstate highway system. The nation's first actual interstate construction took place west of the Missouri River in St. Charles.

The soulless super slab replaced 66, but the old road refused to die. Nostalgia buffs and roadside rebels continued to seek out the tourist traps, motels, and gas stations that still held on for life on 66. People clung to memories of childhood vacations. They kept the "Mother Road" alive.

Route 66 is more than a road. It is a state of mind. It is for those who feel that the journey is half the fun. The 66 traveler seeks out the greasy spoon or the mom-and-pop motel instead of the fast-food joints and motel franchises clustered at the freeway off-ramp. History one can touch is still out there waiting. Just slow down a little and take the next exit.

One

HISTORIC OR SOUTHERN ROUTE FROM 1933 TO 1975

Of all the routes 66 took through St. Louis, the historic or southern route was the most famous, although it actually was not the main route during the halcyon years. From the MacArthur Bridge, Route 66 headed west on Chouteau Avenue to Twelfth Street, Gravois Avenue, Chippewa Street, and Watson Road. The 1926 alignment via the McKinley Bridge and Manchester Road (see chapter 2) was designated as Optional 66. On January 1, 1936, the main route shifted to the Chain of Rocks Bridge (see chapter 3). The route via Chouteau, Twelfth, Gravois, and Chippewa was designated as City 66. The original 1926 alignment kept an Optional 66 designation until 1937. Another City 66 ran from the Chain of Rocks Bridge via Riverview Drive, Broadway, Calvary Avenue, Florissant Avenue, Hebert Street, Thirteenth Street, and Twelfth Street/Tucker Boulevard. In 1955, U.S. 66 moved to the Veteran's Memorial (King) Bridge to the Third Street Expressway (Interstate 55) to the city route at Gravois. City 66 was eliminated in 1963. But when 66 moved to the Poplar Street Bridge in 1967, the main line came back to Gravois, Chippewa, and Watson. Those signs came down in February 1975, and 66 shifted to Interstate 44 until decertification in 1977.

The Municipal Bridge opened in 1916, the first free crossing of the Mississippi River at St. Louis. In 1942, the bridge was renamed in honor of Gen. Douglas MacArthur. Note the treacherous bend on the St. Louis approach. The bridge carried 66 from 1929 to 1935, and City 66 from 1936 to 1955. It closed to automobile traffic in 1981.

Work began on the Veteran's Memorial Bridge in 1948, and it opened on January 13, 1951. At the time, it was the largest cantilever-type bridge over the Mississippi and the sixth-largest cantilever structure in the country. The main line of U.S. 66 used the bridge from 1955 to 1967. The bridge was renamed for Dr. Martin Luther King Jr. in 1972.

World's Largest, Finest Excursion Steamer
S.S. ADMIRAL
on the Mississippi at St. Louis

From 1940 until 1979, the gleaming 342-foot-long SS *Admiral* was a familiar sight gliding beneath the bridges. The ballroom aboard the largest inland steamship in the United States could hold 2,000 dancers. But the engines are gone, and the interior was stripped when it was converted into a now-struggling casino. The *Admiral* faces an uncertain future.

On November 9, 1967, Route 66 was moved onto its fifth and last Mississippi River crossing. The Poplar Street Bridge carried 66 until the end in 1977. It is officially known as the Bernard Dickmann Bridge, after the visionary mayor who pushed for the Jefferson Expansion Memorial. Today the traffic-clogged bridge carries Interstates 55, 70, and 64.

By the Route 66 era, St. Louis had turned its back on the riverfront. The area was filled with grimy tenements and warehouses. Work started to clear the buildings for the riverfront memorial in 1939. But funding problems and haggling over payment to relocate railroad tracks delayed construction of the Gateway Arch until 1963. (Courtesy of the Library of Congress.)

Rising 630 feet above the Mississippi River, the Gateway Arch is the nation's tallest national monument. Eero Saarinen designed it. Two unique "creeper cranes" were raised along sections of track up the side of the arch during construction and are visible in this photograph. The last piece was put in place on October 28, 1965.

By 1966, downtown had a new look. In the foreground is Busch Memorial Stadium, site of the 1966 all-star game as well as the 1967, 1968, 1982, 1985, 1987, and 2004 World Series. Busch also housed football's Cardinals from 1966 to 1987 and the Rams for part of 1995. It was torn down for a new Busch Stadium, which opened in 2006.

Construction on what is now the old courthouse began in 1839 and was finished in 1862. In 1847, the first three trials in the Dred Scott case took place here. Scott was a slave who sued for his freedom after his owner took him to a free state. The U.S. Supreme Court eventually ruled that slaves were not citizens and therefore could not sue. (Courtesy of the Library of Congress.)

This 1957 view shows the Third Street Expressway (66) passing the Basilica of St. Louis, commonly known as the "Old Cathedral." The church was completed in 1834. In 1961, Pope John XXIII designated the cathedral as a basilica. The Old Cathedral was the only building left standing when the riverfront was cleared for the Jefferson Expansion Memorial.

The Hotel York at Sixth and Market Streets boasted that it was on Highways 40, 50, 66, and 67. During the 1940s, rates for the 225 rooms ranged from $2.50 for a single to $6 for a family with two double beds. Dinner in the coffee shop started at 75¢. The Hilton St. Louis at the Ballpark stands on this block today.

Built for the 1904 world's fair, the Jefferson Hotel at Twelfth and Locust Streets had 800 rooms. In 1925, federal officials meeting here designated the highway between Chicago and Los Angeles as U.S. 60. The Jefferson was later a Hilton and a Sheraton hotel. The last guest checked out on July 23, 1975. The Jefferson Arms is now a retirement community.

This view of Market Street looking toward City 66 is dominated by the Civil Courts Building, completed in June 1930. The top level is a replica of the tomb of King Mausolus, built in 352 BC at Halicarnassus in Asia Minor and one of the original Seven Wonders of the Ancient World. It is topped with two 12-foot-tall aluminum griffins.

This view looks north on 12th Street (now Tucker Boulevard) from Market Street. In the background is the Missouri Pacific Building. It was intended to have 35 floors, but the Great Depression halted construction at 23 stories in 1929. The building is now being developed into condominiums. To the right is the curved facade of the Shell Oil building, completed in 1926. (Courtesy of the Missouri State Archives.)

The St. Louis City Hall, at Twelfth and Market Streets, faces Memorial Plaza. The first mail ever carried by air left aboard a balloon from City Hall Square on July 1, 1859. The present building took 14 years to construct and opened in 1904. It is modeled after the Hotel de Ville, the old city hall of Paris, France. The towers were removed in 1936.

The Mart Building at Twelfth and Spruce Streets was built by the Terminal Railroad Association in 1931. It housed the studios of KMOX radio, the "Voice of St. Louis," from 1932 to 1959 and is now the Robert Young Federal Building. Young served in Congress from 1977 to 1987. The building houses the offices of several federal agencies.

St. Francis De Sales Church at Gravois Avenue and Ohio Street is known as the "Cathedral of South St. Louis" because of its 300-foot-tall spire. It is the only church in the area of Gothic German design. The great tornado of 1896 destroyed the previous building, and this structure was completed in 1908. It is now the St. Francis De Sales Oratory.

Edmond's was located at 3185 Gravois Avenue. The "Home of Unusual Sea Foods" was recommended by Duncan Hines and promised the "largest variety of sea food in the Middle West" with shipments arriving daily from all coasts. The 1946 AAA directory says it was "one of the best."

The ultramodern Southtown Famous-Barr at Chippewa Street (City 66) and Kingshighway opened in 1951. The landmark was demolished in 1994 to make room for a big-box home store that was never built. The highly visible 15-acre site sat vacant until 2005. A suburban-style strip mall has since been constructed here. (Photograph by Gerald R. Massie, St. Louis Chamber of Commerce.)

Hampton Village is the oldest shopping center in St. Louis. Harold Brinkop developed the market here for farmers and merchants in 1939. Bettendorf's built one of the city's first supermarkets here in 1940. The Colonial-style stores and offices went up in 1946. From 1950 to 1962, the center even extended to the east side of Hampton Avenue. (Photograph by Gerald R. Massie, St. Louis Chamber of Commerce.)

Bauer's Ranch House at 5805 Chippewa Street was originally known as Telthorst's. Its slogan was "A Bit of the West — Just East of Hampton." Patrons could dine inside their cars or in the "quaint western atmosphere of our beautiful Trophy Dining Room," shown on this postcard. The building is now an ophthalmologist office.

Joseph Mittino's Shangri-La opened in 1940 at 6600 Chippewa Street. "The Club Beautiful" offered fine food and dancing nightly. In 1946, one could get a deluxe steak dinner for $2.75 and enjoy Grace Niggli at the organ. It was later known as Parente's Italian Village, then Saro's Sunny Italy, and now Garavelli's.

Ted Drewes Sr. was an ace tennis player, winning the Muny Championship each year from 1926 to 1935. He started out selling frozen custard from the back of a truck before opening a stand in Florida in 1929. He returned to St. Louis to open a stand on Natural Bridge Avenue in 1930. Drewes is pictured here outside the second store on South Grand Avenue, which opened in 1931. (Ted Drewes Jr.)

No visit to St. Louis is complete without visiting the Ted Drewes location on Route 66. This view was taken shortly after it opened in 1941. The treat is best eaten as a "concrete," basically a shake so thick it can be turned upside down. In the winter, Ted Jr. converts the stand into a lot selling quality Christmas trees. (Ted Drewes Jr.)

John Carr began building the Coral Court Motel at 7755 Watson Road in 1941. Adolph Streubig designed the streamline moderne motel featuring honey-colored bricks and windows of large glass blocks. After World War II, another 23 buildings designed by Harold Tyrer were added with 46 rooms. Three more nondescript buildings in the back added in 1953 brought the total number of rooms to 77.

The Coral Court gained a racy reputation because the rooms with private garages could be rented for four to eight hours, a service originally intended to allow truckers to rest. It closed in 1993 and came down in June 1995. The stone walls at the entrance still stand. One unit was partially reconstructed at the Museum of Transportation on Barrett Station Road.

The Wayside Auto Court still stands across from the Coral Court site. It had 33 brick cottages and advertised "Commercial Men Welcome." The outside at least still retains a feel of the old road. The site of the Coral Court and the Wayside are in the village of Marlborough, best known for being a speed trap.

The Chippewa Motel at 7880 Watson Road still stands as apartments. But it is not a place where one would want to hang around. The 13 freestanding units, called "tourist cottages," opened in 1937. They rented for $1.50 per night, complete with running water and access to community toilets and shower. The cottages were later joined to form 20 units.

The Duplex Motel at 7898 Watson Road also opened in 1937. It still stands and has also been converted to apartments. Originally there were 11 cottages with private toilets and room radios for $2.50 per night. By the time Jack and Bernice Holloway were running it in 1971, the Duplex had 27 units.

Missouri Motel
City Route Hwy 66
2 Miles West of St. Louis

The Missouri Motel at 8084 Watson Road was constructed in 1950 and obviously took its styling from the Coral Court. It also included attached garages. This card says the "Ultra Modern" motel offered hot-water heat, television, and air-conditioning. One of a string of office buildings west of Laclede Station Road occupies the site today.

The Cordia Courts at 8498 Watson Road were "as Modern as Tomorrow" and offered "automatic heat, air cooled, locked garages and free radios." The motor court was built in the 1940s. It later became the Motel U.S. Grant, which worked out nicely since it was at the corner of Watson Road and General Grant Lane. The site is now an office park.

The 66 Auto Court had 30 rooms, billed as "the Finest Modern Auto Court" in the St. Louis area. The 1946 AAA directory calls it "pleasant." Since the court was three miles west of the city limits, the slogan asked, "Why Spend the Night in the City?" The card noted that the 66 was still only 15 minutes from downtown.

This view of a room at the 66 Auto Court shows what $2.50 per night bought travelers back in 1946. The complex had 30 rooms, each with "hot water heat, insulated rooms, innerspring mattresses, electric fans," and "city water." The Watson Auto Care Plaza occupies this site at 8730 Watson Road today.

Otto Mayer built the Evergreen Cabins at 8723 Watson Road in the early 1940s. There were 14 double brick cabins, which were bought by Allie and Alvena Langbein in 1948. Emil Wildermuth owned the cabins from 1960 until they closed down in 1968. The Evergreen Apartments are located here today.

Motel Royal, the "Travelers Paradise," had 60 rooms with each facing a beautiful landscaped private parkway. The St. Louis Chamber of Commerce used a photograph of the Motel Royal as an example of the fine motels here. Recommended by AAA, each room had an attached garage. Coldwell Banker Gundaker Real Estate is now at 9282 Watson Road.

The Oaks Motel and package liquor store was at 9285 Watson Road and stood until the late 1960s. The liquor store offered "choice wines liquors and beers, along with tobacco, candy and novelties." The motel had 16 rooms, complete with porter and maid service. A bank occupies this site today.

Flexor Drive Ins opened the Route 66 Park In at 9438 Watson Road back in 1947. Wehrenberg took over the following year. The parking lot could hold 800 cars, and moviegoers could also enjoy free pony rides, a Ferris wheel, and even a trained bear cub. The back of the giant screen was bathed in neon, making it impossible to miss from the highway.

In this photograph, a police cruiser lurks behind the 66 marquee touting the March 1958 release *Dragstrip Riot*. The studios of legendary rock radio station KSHE were located next door. The 66 was torn down in 1994 to make room for a National (now Schnuck's) Supermarket and other stores. (Photograph by Gerald R. Massie, Missouri State Archives.)

"New Rooms Sleep Keen, see us for old fashioned rates," says the back of this card for the Bel-Air Motel, immediately adjacent to Crestwood Plaza. Amenities included "TV, radio, Garage, air conditioning, credit cards, dining room and coffee shop." An office building stands here at 9745 Watson Road today.

The Colonial Rooms and Efficiency Apartments offered hourly bus service to St. Louis and to "Sylvian" Beach on the Meremec River. The Colonial later became the Alexander and Sons Funeral Home, which was torn down in the 1980s. The Crestwood Theatre was built on the site, and Watson Plaza replaced the theater in 1986.

BLUE HAVEN
4 MI. W. ST. LOUIS, Mo.
ON HWY. 66,

The Blue Haven Motel at 10000 Watson Road started out as a private home in the early 1940s. It grew to 24 units with spacious grounds. Sol Schlansky owned it from 1955 to 1975, when it was torn down. According to Skip Curtis in *The Missouri U.S. 66 Tour Book*, Schlansky raised chickens on the property. A medical office now stands here.

Blue Bonnet Court
4½ Miles West of
St. Louis
Missouri

SLEEP AND REST   IN THE BEST

On U. S. City 66 - One half Mile East of By pass at Junction of U. S. 66 and 61

Constructed in 1938, the Blue Bonnet Court at 10100 Watson Road invited travelers to "Sleep and Rest in the Best." There were originally 18 brick cottages, renting from $2 to $3 and "individually heated with modern oil heat, the fumes of which are carried off by vents." Johnny Mac's Sporting Goods opened on the site in the mid-1960s.

Twin-Six Auto Court, 10,230 Hwy. 66, St. Louis 22, Mo.

The "Ultra Modern tourist cottages" of the Twin-Six Auto Court were built about 1940 by the Sinwell brothers. The rooms were "Simmons Furnished." A. W. Aschinger bought the place in 1969, and it was torn down in 1986. A Bank of America branch is located here at 10230 Watson Road today.

The Westward Motel, "One of the Nation's Finest," occupied the northeast part of the Watson Road and Lindbergh Boulevard interchange until just a few years ago. The sign was salvaged and shines once again at the Museum of Transportation, right next to the restored partial unit of the Coral Court. A Hampton Inn was built on the site.

The first cloverleaf interchange west of the Mississippi River opened on August 21, 1931, at Watson Road and Lindbergh Boulevard. The pink granite bridge was where the route around the city of St. Louis (1933–1955 main line 66, 1955–1965 bypass) connected with the southern or historic route. The bridge was replaced in 1980. (Photograph by Gerald R. Massie, Missouri State Archives.)

The Park Plaza Court were located on the northwest side of the Watson Road and Lindbergh Boulevard interchange. The hotel grew to 135 rooms and became known as the Ozark Plaza Motor Hotel before it was torn down. It was part of a chain that operated similarly styled motels on Route 66 in Flagstaff, Arizona, and in Tulsa, Oklahoma. Note the cheerleader.

Nelson's Cafe was part of the Park Plaza Court complex. It became the Flame Restaurant sometime before the Holiday Inn opened next door in 1960. The complex is now known as the Holiday Inn Southwest–Viking Conference Center. There are currently plans to redevelop the site for offices and retail. (Photograph by Gerald R. Massie, Missouri State Archives.)

The Flame Restaurant (previously Nelson's, later the Viking) called itself "St. Louis County's Most Gracious Dining and Drinking Establishment" at "the Crossroads of the Nation—Kirkwood, Missouri." It was home to the Golden Peacock Lounge and Key Banquet Room. This is all part of the Holiday Inn complex today.

Sylvan Beach Park sprang up in the 1930s at a rare spot on the Meramec River where it was safe to swim. The complex also had a big swimming pool, picnic areas, baseball diamonds, pony rides, and horseback riding. One trail ran to a cave that could hold 26 horses. Most of it was torn down in 1954 for construction of the Interstate 44 bridges.

Sunset Ranch Motel offered "blond oak furniture, soft water and electric heating" as well as a couple of playgrounds and a service station. The Park 'n Eat Restaurant was adjacent to the motel. The Sunset Ranch was part of a strip of hotels along South Highway Drive, a handful of which stood in run-down condition into the 1990s.

ROSE LAWN MOTEL – U.S. HIGHWAY'S 66 & 50 – KIRKWOOD – ST. LOUIS CO., MO.

The Rose Lawn Motel was constructed in 1955 and "built 200 feet off the highway for restful sleeping." The "Ultra Modern" motel offered soft filtered water, tile baths, hot-water radiant heat, large rooms, and a children's playground. The First Academy Child Care Center occupies this site at 570 South Highway Drive today.

On July 1, 1959, the new $50 million Chrysler plant on Highway 66 began operation. Plymouths, Dodge Darts, and Chrysler's compact Valiant were the first cars produced here. At the time, St. Louis was the second-largest producer of automobiles in the nation. The truck plant next door opened in 1966.

Hungry folks gulp sliders here today. A White Castle restaurant occupies the site of Dudley's Cabins and Service, near what is now Interstate 44 and Bowles Avenue. A postcard said, "We service your car while you sleep." Mr. Dudley was a well-known moonshiner. In the 1950s, the complex was known as the Jam Inn.

Hill-Top Motel

VALLEY PARK, MO.

The Hill-Top Motel was at the top of the hill one mile west of the Chrysler plant and a half mile east of Missouri 141. The Hill-Top offered ranch-style construction, new and modern large rooms, and comfortable beds. It was also "Air conditioned by Refrigeration" and offered "reasonable rates."

"HALINAR'S CAFE & CABINS"

Delicious Foods   **Highway No. 66**   9 Miles West of ST. LOUIS MO

The site of Halinar's Cafe is now part of the Maritz campus. The company headquarters along the section of Route 66 once known as the Henry Shaw Gardenway are beautifully landscaped. Maritz is the world's largest single source of integrated performance improvement, travel, and marketing research services.

THE QUONSET SERVICE STATION & CAFE
10 Miles West of St. Louis on Highway 66
One of Missouri's Better Truck Stops

After World War II, the military found itself with thousands of Quonset huts. They were sold as surplus for $1,000 each and were perfect for roadside businesses. The Quonset Service Station and Cafe used three of them. The huts were named for Quonset Point in Rhode Island, where they were first assembled.

TRAV-O-TEL AUTO COURT
Valley Park, Mo.

MEMBER NATIONAL
TRAV-O-TEL-SYSTEM

Steam Heat   Electric Fans

U. S. HIGHWAY NO. 66
11 MILES WEST OF ST. LOUIS

A 1939 AAA guide says the Trav-O-Tel Auto Court at the intersection of the Old Antire Road was one of the finest in the St. Louis area. Operated in the 1940s by Mr. and Mrs. A. Ott, the motel was part of an early chain. There were 16 brick cottages with "broadloom rugs and closed rock garages." The site is a vacant field today.

This section of 66 between St. Louis and the Shaw Arboretum in Gray Summit was designated as the Henry Shaw Gardenway in honor of the founder of the Missouri Botanical Garden. This 1934 view shows homeless men planting some of the wide variety of trees that lines the route. (Courtesy of the Missouri State Archives.)

Beecher's Log Cabin stood near a government ammunition storage facility later converted to a vast green space. Tyson Valley now includes Lone Elk Park, West Tyson Park, the Tyson Research Center, the World Bird Sanctuary, and the Wild Canid Survival and Research Center, better known as the Wolf Sanctuary.

The Bridgehead Inn opened in 1935 and became a haven for gambling and other illicit activities. Edward Steinberg took over in 1947, cleaned things up, and ran Steiny's here until 1972. The restaurant was later known as the Galley West and served as the EPA headquarters during the cleanup of Times Beach. It now houses the Route 66 State Park visitor's center. (Courtesy of the Missouri State Archives.).

Times Beach was founded in 1925, when the *St. Louis Star-Times* offered a 20-by-100-foot lot for $67.50 with a subscription. Waste oil was sprayed on the dusty streets in the 1970s. After a disastrous flood in December 1982, residents learned the oil was tainted with dioxin. The EPA leveled the town and burned the dioxin in a controversial incinerator. The cleaned-up site was reborn as Route 66 State Park on September 11, 1999.

CAPE COD CABINS · U.S. 66 EUREKA MISSOURI.

Cap eCod Cabins were located on the western edge of Times Beach and were open until the late 1960s. The sign reads, "Vacancy / Drive-In / Showers." At this end of Route 66 State Park, the old road can be seen disappearing under Interstate 44. The 419-acre park is now a haven for wildlife and offers level trails for bikers and pedestrians.

Deek Keeton built the Rock City Cafe, cabins and gas station between the Frisco and Missouri Pacific tracks. Ed LaMar's Ozark Cafe and tourist court, tavern and gas station were immediately to the east. The buildings were similar, so both businesses became known as Rock City. It was all torn down for I-44 in 1955.

Eureka has changed a great deal since this view of the new four-lane Route 66 was made in 1956. The opening of Six Flags Over Mid America amusement park spurred a major building boom. The Sinclair station at far right was originally Gerwe's Log House Cafe. It was owned by former major league baseball player Bob Klinger and leased to Lou Gerwe. Gerwe's later became Don and Dot Hanephin's Log House Café.

Gerwes Log House Cafe offered "good food at all hrs." The 1934 Eureka High School building is in the background. *Eureka* is from the Greek, meaning "I have found it." In 1853, an engineer for the Pacific Railroad named a construction camp here Eureka after discovering an easy path for the rails through the valley.

The Al-Pac was built in 1942, combining the names Allenton and Pacific. "President Fred A. Miller and his "first lady and resident manager" Jean Miller were proud of their beautiful cedar dining room. The restaurant portion became a lounge and burned down in 1976, but part of the lodge and motel they added on later still stands.

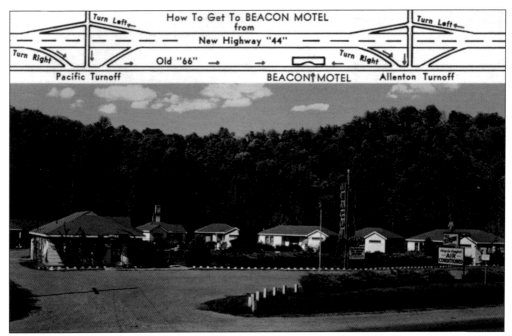

The Beacon Court opened in 1946 with "14 Modern, Inviting, Tastefully Decorated Cottages." The owners placed a beacon atop an old windmill derrick converted into a sign. The motel closed in the early 1980s but George and Monica Mahler restored the sign and placed it at their Beacon Car Wash. Part of the complex still stands and houses a towing company.

Former bootleggers James and Bill Smith built the Red Cedar Inn in 1934 with logs from their farm. They added the bar addition in 1935. James II and Katherine Smith closed the Red Cedar in 1973, but Ginger and James Smith III restored and ran it from 1987 until March 7, 2005. The City of Pacific is reportedly considering buying the property for a museum.

In 1939, a stone overlook was dedicated on Highway 66 east of Pacific in honor of Peter Lars Jensen. The longtime director of the nearby Shaw Arboretum was president of the Henry Shaw Gardenway Association, directing the beautification of Highway 66 between the St. Louis city limits and the arboretum.

This view from the overlook actually looks much the same today. A steam train is just entering the picture from the west. These tracks carried the Frisco and the Missouri Pacific Railroads. The Missouri Pacific Railroad merged with Union Pacific Railroad in 1997. The Frisco Railroad was synonymous with Route 66 in Missouri until merging with Burlington Northern Railroad in 1980.

Silica has been mined in Pacific since the 1870s. The bluffs along Route 66 are riddled with massive caves created by the miners. The silica was used to make fine glassware and is also used in bricks and cleansers. Today businesses use many of the caves for storage because the temperature inside stays at 60 degrees year-round.

Pacific was originally incorporated as Franklin in 1852. But there was already a Franklin in Missouri, and constant mix-ups in the mail required a name change. The Missouri Pacific Railroad arrived in 1853, and the name was changed in 1859. The new Route 66 through town opened in 1933.

Two

THE 1926–1932 ORIGINAL ROUTE

Route 66 originally crossed the Mississippi River on the McKinley Bridge, then followed Ninth Street, Salisbury Street, Natural Bridge Avenue, Grand Avenue, Delmar Boulevard, Sarah Street, Lindell Boulevard, Boyle Avenue, Clayton Avenue, and McCausland Avenue before turning west on Manchester Road. In 1929, Route 66 shifted to the Municipal or "Free Bridge" (now the MacArthur). The route then followed Seventh Street to Chouteau Avenue, angled onto Manchester Road, and then turned onto Boyle Avenue, Clayton Avenue, McCausland Avenue, and Manchester Road. Other guides have the route as Salisbury, Natural Bridge, Grand, Delmar, Sarah, Lindell, Skinker Boulevard, and McCausland to Manchester. The route over the McKinley Bridge was marked as Optional 66. The new highway through Valley Park to Gray Summit opened on August 5, 1933. Merchants along Manchester fought in vain to have the new road designated as Optional 66. But Manchester became U.S. 50 and is now Missouri 100.

8748. McKinley Bridge, St. Louis, Mo.

The McKinley Bridge was built in 1910. The bridge is not named for the U.S. president but for Congressman William B. McKinley. He was president of the interurban railroad that constructed the bridge. The span was closed for an overhaul in 2001 and finally reopened in December 2007. It now includes a pedestrian and bike path.

The Fairgrounds Hotel
OPPOSITE BEAUTIFUL FAIRGROUNDS PARK
SAINT LOUIS, MO.
ON U.S. HIGHWAY 40-66

HOLLAND TAVERN

Some of the greatest baseball players of all time stayed at the Fairgrounds Hotel at Natural Bridge Avenue and Grand Avenue. Stan Musial lived here as a rookie in 1941. Huge yearly fairs were held across the street at Fairgrounds Park from 1856 to 1902. The park included a horse-racing track that could hold 25,000 fans and the city's first zoo.

Sportsmen's Park was at Grand Avenue and Dodier Street. The Browns played here from 1902 to 1953, and it was the home of the Cardinals from 1925 to 1966. The football Cardinals played their games here from 1960 to 1965. Sportsmen's was renamed Busch Stadium in 1953 and torn down in 1966. The Herbert Hoover Boys and Girls Club occupies the site today.

The Ralston-Purina Corporation headquarters at Chouteau Avenue and Twelfth Street was known around the world as "Checkerboard Square." The company made Chex cereal, Purina dog food, Energizer batteries, and many other products. Many of those product lines have been spun off, and Ralston-Purina merged with Nestle in 2001.

The Coronado Hotel at 3701 Lindell Boulevard opened in 1925. The guest list included Harry Truman, Charles Lindbergh, Rudolph Valentino, and Queen Marie of Romania. The hotel closed in 1965, and the building sat vacant for several years. A $40 million renovation in 2003 restored its former glory. The grand ballroom is breathtaking.

In the early days, the Automobile Club of Missouri placed the markers along the U.S. routes. All four passing through St. Louis in 1926 (40, 50, 61, and 66) were routed past the AAA headquarters in an old mansion at 4228 Lindell Boulevard. This building a few blocks east with its landmark giant thermometer housed AAA from 1938 to 1975.

50

Work began on the "new" cathedral at Lindell Boulevard and Newstead Avenue on May 1, 1907. The cathedral was consecrated on June 29, 1926. Work on the interior and mosaics continued until 1988. The dome was inspired by the Church of Hagia Sophia in Constantinople. In 1997, Pope John Paul II designated the cathedral as a basilica.

ART MUSEUM, FOREST PARK, ST. LOUIS MO.

Forest Park opened on June 24, 1876, and covers 1,293 acres, 450 more than Central Park in New York. The art museum is a remnant from the 1904 world's fair, which drew 20 million visitors to the park. In front of the museum atop Art Hill stands a statue of the city namesake, King Louis IX.

The Forest Park Highlands, within sight of Route 66 on Oakland Avenue, began with a simple merry-go-round in 1896. It grew to include two roller coasters. Other rides included the Racer Dip and the Flying Turns. There was a big pool, a dance hall, and a funhouse. A huge fire in 1963 destroyed nearly everything, and Forest Park Community College stands here today.

The Arena opened in 1929, intended as the permanent home for the National Dairy Show before the promoters went bankrupt. The St. Louis Blues of the NHL played here from 1967 until 1994. The "Old Barn" hosted concerts by artists from Frank Sinatra to Michael Jackson. It came down on February 27, 1999, to make room for an office complex.

The building at 9243 Manchester Road is one of the oldest continually operated taverns in St. Louis County. Originally known as the Nine-Mile House, it was Porta's Tavern from 1932 to 1982. In July 1982, George and Kris Hansford opened the Trainwreck Saloon. The original back bar is still there, and a real caboose occupies the beer garden.

Buckingham's Restaurant advertised "Table d'Hote," or family-style dinners, "where polite people assemble." It was originally a private residence, converted to a restaurant in the 1920s. This building still stands on the north side of Manchester Road, west of Annalee Avenue.

Constructed in 1940, the Manchester Drive-In was one of the first in the area. It was torn down in 1967 to make room for West County Center. The mall's symbol was a giant dove logo perched on a pole high above Manchester Road and Interstate 270. The landmark was preserved when the mall was renovated.

Henry K. Pierce envisioned a chain of grandiose facilities every 125 miles in the Ozarks, at a time when roadside services were rudimentary. The Pierce-Pennant facility at Des Peres opened on July 27, 1929, on the south side of Manchester Road, immediately west of where Interstate 270 is today. Pennant also operated lavish terminals in Rolla; Springfield; Miami, Oklahoma; and Tulsa, Oklahoma.

Heggs Tourist camp east of Missouri 141 was one of the first to spring up when Manchester was designated as Route 66. The postcard noted that the camp offered "some cottages equipped with hot and cold running water" with "Gas and groceries in connection." The West County Auto Plaza is located here now.

AN ENTRANCE TO RESTAURANT AND TOURIST CABINS—BIG CHIEF HOTEL
ON HIGHWAY 50 AND 66 AT POND, MO., P. O. ADDRESS CENTAUR, MO.

The Pierce-Pennant Petroleum Company opened the Big Chief in 1929. The 60 units with attached garages originally rented for $3. The restaurant offered a 75¢ steak dinner. In 1993, it became the Big Chief Dakota grill, offering bison burgers, elk, and even alligator. B. Donovan's Restaurant opened here at 17352 Manchester in 2006.

Rudy and Edna Dehn opened the Motor Inn on the original Manchester Road alignment (now Missouri 100) at Gray Summit around 1927. The sign advertises 10¢ hamburgers and roast beef, pork, or baked ham sandwiches for 15¢. A plate lunch set customers back 30¢. The building stood until the 1960s.

Mr. and Mrs. Clifford Weirich were the owners of the Cozy Dine restaurant and gas station in Gray Summit. They offered Shell gasoline under the classic sign that simply says "Eats." There were sleeping rooms available in the brick home. The home is still there, but the restaurant building no longer stands.

Three

BYPASS ROUTE USED FROM 1936 TO 1965

The main route of Route 66 was moved to cross the Chain of Rocks Bridge as of January 1, 1935. AASHTO designated the main route of 66 as "beginning at the Mississippi River west of Mitchell, via State Route 77 (Dunn, Lindbergh) to Pattonville, then coincide with U.S. 61 to a point south of Kirkwood." This route received the Bypass 66 designation in 1955, when the main line moved to the King Bridge. Interstate 270 between Interstate 70 and Riverview Drive carried the Bypass 66-40 designation from its opening on October 3, 1962, until the bypass was discontinued on October 2, 1965.

The Chain of Rocks Bridge opened in 1929. It carried Route 66 from 1936 to 1955 and Bypass 66 from 1955 to 1965. The bridge was originally painted silver, but the War Department ordered the olive drab paint in 1942 to make the bridge less visible from the air. Traffic fell to a trickle when the Interstate 270 bridge to the north opened on September 1, 1966.

CHAIN OF ROCKS BRIDGE
St. Louis, Mo.

Where U. S. 66, "Will Rogers Highway", crosses the Mississippi River

The bridge closed in 1970, and only a drop in scrap metal prices kept it from being torn down. The Chain of Rocks subbed for postapocalyptic New York in the cheesy 1981 movie *Escape from New York*. Gateway Trailnet gave the landmark a new lease on life, reopening it as a link in a network of biking and hiking trails in June 1999.

Mark Twain described the St. Louis drinking water as "too thick to drink and too thin to plow." The Chain of Rocks Water Works was the largest in the United States when it opened in 1894. But the filtration process was not perfected until just before the 1904 world's fair. The beautifully landscaped bluff above became a favorite recreation spot.

CHAIN OF ROCKS AMUSEMENT PARK — 10783 RIVERVIEW DRIVE — ST. LOUIS, MO.

By 1927, an amusement park had sprung up on the bluff. Chain of Rocks Amusement Park boasted a hand-carved 46-horse carousel, a huge swimming pool, and the Swooper, which resembled an oval Ferris wheel. This view shows the Comet roller coaster, a wooden coaster complete with protruding nails. The Comet was torn down in 1958.

59

The park later was known Chain of Rocks Fun Fair. Nearly every school in north St. Louis County held picnics here. The park was doomed when Six Flags Over Mid-America opened in 1971. Chain of Rocks Fun Fair held on until Labor Day 1977. St. Louis became the first major U.S. city without an amusement park.

The two structures below the bridge that resemble castles are intake towers for the waterworks. Tower No. 1 was designed by William S. Eames in the Romanesque style and built in 1894. A dike once ran out to the tower. Tower No. 2 is designed to resemble a Roman villa. It was designed by Roth and Study and constructed in 1915.

Route 66 originally did not use the Chain of Rocks Bridge, partly because there were no decent highways across northern St. Louis County. This April 1933 view shows the new Missouri 77 and Missouri 99. In 1935, Route 77 became Route 66. Route 99 became 367, and this quiet scene is now the Interstate 270 and Missouri 367 interchange. (Courtesy of the Missouri State Archives.)

St. Louis philanthropist John Myers designed this Palladian-style summer home but died before it was completed in 1869. His widow, Adelaide, oversaw the construction. The house at 180 Dunn Road was nearly torn down for construction of the Interstate 170/Interstate 270 interchange. It currently houses craft stores and is reported to be haunted. (Courtesy of Rosemary Davidson.)

Carl and Della Mae Riegel owned the Wayfarer Inn Motel and Dining Room when this view was taken in 1961. The 66-unit Wayfarer offered "Wired Music" and the AAA guide for 1966–1967 says the motel offered "very pleasant, attractive, well-kept rooms." The building at 8911 Dunn Road is now the Budget Host Inn.

The Knotty Pine Tourist Lodge, "¼ mile east of the Lincoln-Mercury Plant," boasted modern cabins with "showers, radio and heat" in every unit. It was constructed in the 1930s at Route 66 and Taylor Road. The little motel at 9015 Dunn Road managed to hang on until 1987. The Apache Village RV and camper dealership occupies the site today.

Mr. and Mrs. Ed Holtzman opened the Airport Motel at 6221 Lindbergh Boulevard in 1936, and it is still in operation today. One of the front units is now a barbershop. The hotel with "ranch house deluxe cabins, best in the Midwest" once had a great sign featuring a big blue neon airplane. The sign is one of the few things that have changed.

Henry Ford's grandson Benson dedicated the Ford plant on September 21, 1948. Hazelwood was founded when Florissant tried to annex the new plant in 1949. Workers built Ford and Mercury automobiles until 1984. The plant then built the Ford Explorer and Mercury Mountaineer before closing in March 2006.

James S. McDonnell founded his aircraft company in 1939 with one employee. By 1980, over 40,000 people worked there. McDonnell built the famous F-4 Phantom, the F-15 Eagle, and the F/A-18 Hornet. The *Mercury* and *Gemini* space capsules were built here. McDonnell merged with Douglas Aircraft in 1967 and with Boeing in 1996. This 1953 lineup of McDonnell-produced aircraft highlights advances in jet fighters since the production of the first Phantom in August 1945. From left to right are an FH-1 Phantom, the navy's first all-jet carrier-based fighter; the F2H-4, the latest of the navy Banshee series; the air force XF-88B, used for research on supersonic turboprop propellers; and the F3H-1 Demon.

Route 66 cuts across the left side in this 1934 view of Lambert Field. Maj. Albert Bond Lambert developed the airfield at his own expense and then sold it to the city at the price he paid for the land alone. Charles Lindbergh flew the mail from here. He persuaded some local businessmen to finance his flight in the *Spirit of St. Louis*.

The original Lambert Field terminal opened in 1933, facing Lindbergh Boulevard on the north side of the airport. The "Union Station of the Air" could handle four planes at once. When it opened, there were no runways, just a grass field and concrete taxiways to the terminal. This terminal was replaced in 1956 and torn down in 1979.

Mayor Raymond Tucker dedicated the new Lambert Field terminal on the south side of the airport and along Interstate 70 on March 10, 1956. Minoru Yamasaki, George Hellmuth, and Joseph Leinweber came up with an innovative design featuring three thin shell concrete domes. There are now four. Yamasaki went on to design the World Trade Center.

Frank and Edna Bulan's Ultra Modern Hotel was at 5024 North Lindbergh Boulevard. There were 17 brick units with tile showers, Beauty Rest beds, telephones, free television, and a radio in every room. There was also a restaurant here. Their telephone number was Terryhill 5-2970. The hotel was torn down for airport expansion.

Motel St. Louis, the "Motel Beautiful," was at 5028 North Lindbergh Boulevard. There were 46 units. That is probably the motel vehicle parked out front because it offered "station wagon service" to the airport. The card says, "You'll be proud to say I Stopped at the new Motel St. Louis." It was torn down in the 1960s.

The 24-unit Alura Motel at 4665 Lindbergh Boulevard later became the Lin-Air Motel. The motel was "air cooled" and also had radiant heat. Today nothing remains of Route 66 or several other businesses between here and Interstate 70. A reconstructed Lindbergh swings to the right of the old route through a high-tech tunnel beneath a new runway.

Stanley Williams built his motel in 1950 at Lindbergh Boulevard and Natural Bridge Avenue. The Apollo One astronauts stayed here while training at McDonnell Aircraft. The neat little court was torn down in 2001 as construction on the tunnel began. The sign can be seen at Rich Henry's Rabbit Ranch in Staunton, Illinois, along with the sign from the Lin-Air Motel.

Billed as "the Finest Motel in St. Louis County," the Sands at 4630 Lindbergh Boulevard was owned and operated by Mr. and Mrs. Paul Lammers in 1960. The complex had 50 units when this view was taken. It grew into the Henry VIII Hotel and Conference Center with 155 rooms and 190 suites. It was all torn down for the runway.

The Holiday Inn at Lindbergh Boulevard and Long Road was the first of the two Holiday Inns on the bypass route. It started off with 150 rooms and grew to 392. This location had a service station, station wagon service to the airport, and "sitters for setters," a kennel service. Later the Bridgeton Clarion, it is now a Ramada Inn.

A 1959 Ford Skyliner is heading from the new Mark Twain Expressway (Interstate 70) onto Bypass 66-67 south. (Lindbergh Boulevard). On August 13, 1956, the first construction under the Interstate Highway Act began just seven miles to the west at Interstate 70 and Missouri Route 94. Missouri is the birthplace of the interstate system that replaced Route 66.

Mr. and Mrs. Michael Rampani owned the Air-O-Way Courts at 4125 Lindbergh Boulevard during its heyday. The 16 "Permastone Cottages" had "city certified water, Spring Air mattresses and blond oak furniture." Harold Jones changed the name to the Air Way in the 1970s. The motel stood into the 1990s and came down for a Home Depot.

This view shows Bypass 66 (from left to right in center) at St. Charles Rock Road in 1964. Pattonville High School is on the left. Work is about to begin on Northwest Plaza on the right. When it opened on August 16, 1965, Louis Zorensky's shopping center was one of the largest in the world. The mall today is a shadow of its former self, a victim of competition and changing demographics. (Courtesy of the Missouri State Archives.)

Sunset Acres stood at 3720 Lindbergh Boulevard. "Member of AAA and Superior Courts," it was owned by Al and Vernon Koch. Mr. and Mrs. Frank J. Lama were running it when this postcard was issued. The card touts "Ultra-modern concessions, Airfoam mattresses, and Mengel Furniture." It was torn down for Northwest Plaza construction.

The Four Star Tourist Court was built in the 1940s, owned and operated by Thomas M. Byrne. It offered "Clean Modern cabins and Fine Foods." The cabins were in the back behind the coffee shop. It was torn down to widen Lindbergh Boulevard, and the site north of Adie Road is now the Lighthouse Baptist Church.

The Ivy Motel was built in the 1950s. The building faced Olive Street Road (Missouri 340) but was promoted as being on the much more famous Route 66. Its motto was Hospitality, Comfort, Economy. The Knotty Pine Court stood across the street until the 1980s. The Ivy is still there at 10143 Old Olive Street.

Originally known as the Smith Brothers Motel, the 33-room King Brothers Motel was located at the intersection of four superhighways, U.S. 40-61 and U.S. 66-67. It was "Under the Supervision of the Automobile Club of America" in 1948 but still gained a notorious reputation. The Frontenac Hilton stands on the site today.

Looking south on Route 66 (Lindbergh Boulevard) from U.S. 40-61, Rapp's Supermarket is on the left with the Heintz Service Station and King Brothers Motel on the right. In 1927, the *Watchman Advocate* newspaper held a contest to find the best way for St. Louis County to honor Charles Lindbergh. John J. Rott won with his suggestion of a highway around the county named in Lindbergh's honor. Lindbergh Boulevard opened in 1931, combining Sappington Barracks Road, Denny Road, and Bridgeton Station Road.

Looking north on Route 66 at Manchester Road on July 9, 1952, on the right are Vernon Jump's Tydol station, Kirkwood Motors Plymouth and DeSoto, and Doerflinger Realtors. Kirkwood Mitsubishi occupies the corner today. A right turn would quickly take travelers to the Hollywood and Sunset Tourist Courts. (Courtesy of the Missouri State Archives.)

Spencer's Grill in the heart of Kirkwood opened on October 14, 1947. William Spencer and his wife, Irene, kept it open 24 hours per day, making the most of the Route 66 traffic. The grill was remodeled in 1948. Most of the fixtures, including the neon sign and clock outside, are from that time. Chris Powers runs Spencer's today. (Courtesy of Chris Powers.)

Established in 1853, Kirkwood was the first planned community west of the Mississippi River and a haven from the pollution and cholera plaguing St. Louis. The "Queen of the Suburbs" is named for the Pacific Railroad's chief engineer and surveyor. The train station constructed in 1893 still serves Amtrak passengers.

Four

FRANKLIN COUNTY

Route 66 climbs slowly out of the valley west of Pacific. At Gray Summit, the highway unites with U.S. 50 for six and a half miles. According to the WPA's 1933 guide to the Show Me State, between the junction and St. Clair "U.S. 66 continues along the approximate route of the Old Wire Road, and traverses the wide, rolling plateau that separates the valleys of the Meramec and Bourbeuese Rivers." West of St. Clair, "the Ozark foothills become sharper, their sheer sides exposing a variety of strata." For miles, tourists would have seen barns painted with advertisements for "the Greatest Show Under the Earth." They were almost there.

Many of the caves created by silica mining were exposed when the bluff was cut back for the new Route 66 in 1932–1933. They inspired the name of the Cave Cafe, which also operated as a tavern for a time. Ralph Martin owned it from 1943 to 1987. The building is still there, occupied by Good Heart Enterprises.

Mr. and Mrs. Walter Cook were managing the O.K. Motel west of Pacific when this view was made. Owner Mittie Morris was murdered at her motel on January 16, 1981, causing locals to call for demolition of the deteriorating motel. Some of the units were moved down the highway, where they are used by a storage business.

THE MULE TRADING POST

HIWAY 66 PACIFIC, MO.

Frank Ebling founded the Mule Trading Post in Pacific in 1946. The billboards featuring a cartoon mule trademark made it one of the most famous souvenir shops in the Ozarks. After Interstate 44 bypassed the Mule, Ebling moved his business to Rolla in 1957. The ear-waggling mule neon sign still greets tourists there today.

Built in 1945, the Trail's End Motel's "modern" heated units with showers were later connected. After Interstate 44 was constructed in 1965, owners Willard and Bernice Haley put up the big vertical Motel sign that is still a landmark. But the court now appears abandoned and is deteriorating quickly, the yard filled with junked cars.

Ed and Dell Moore ran the Crest Restaurant, three miles west of Pacific. "We Specialize in Chicken and Steak Dinners." It was fancy enough to accept reservations, and a chicken plate would set diners back 75¢. The station is selling Texaco gasoline in this view, mailed in 1947. It later sold D-X gas.

This view shows Route 66 looking east from the top of the hill where Missouri 100 meets the old road today at Gray Summit. Gray Summit was originally known as Point Labadie. It was later named for Daniel Gray, who operated a hotel here decades before Route 66. It is the highest point on the railroad between St. Louis and Kansas City.

In 1925, the smoky pall that covered St. Louis was choking the plants at the Missouri Botanical Garden. The Shaw Arboretum was founded to cultivate plants, and in case the garden needed to move. Today known as the Shaw Nature Preserve, its 2,500 acres consist of restored prairies, wetlands, and woodlands. It is open to the public.

This Missouri state weight station was located directly across from the Shaw Arboretum. It handled trucks traveling in both the east- and westbound lanes of Route 66, which caused some major traffic tie-ups. The truck on the scales in this 1942 view was owned by Milligan Grocery in St. Louis. (Courtesy of the St. Clair Historical Museum.)

The Gardenway Motel is still in business today. It takes its name from the Henry Shaw Gardenway and marks the parkway's western end. The sign with its glass block inset is a true classic. Louis Eckelcamp, co-owner of the Diamonds, built the original Gardenway units in the 1940s. The motel promoted 41 units with free television.

In 1919, Spencer Groff set up a stand to sell plums from the family orchard where the Ozark Trail (later Missouri 100) met the Old Springfield Road (later Route 66). A customer said it reminded him of a banana stand, and the name stuck. In the photograph, Groff is marking out the location of a new stand. Notice the shape. (Courtesy of the St. Clair Historical Museum.)

Groff opened a more impressive facility on July 3, 1927. He named it the Diamonds for the way the property was shaped by the intersection. The two swimming pools held "180,000 gallons of fresh running crystal water." The Diamonds was promoted as "the World's Largest Roadside Restaurant," serving one million customers per year.

Restaurant employee Louis Eckelcamp and Nobel Key bought "the Old Reliable Eating Place" in 1935. By then, the complex also included 12 cabins. The cabins eventually grew into the 25-room Mission Bell Motel. This 1939 photograph shows Eckelcamp, his family, and the "75 courteous employees to serve you."

The Diamonds is seen here from the ground in 1955. The Diamonds moved to a new location on Interstate 44 in 1967, and the old sign went too. In 1971, Roscoe and Arla Reed moved their Tri-County Truck Stop from Sullivan to the vacant building. The Tri-County Truck Stop continued to serve travelers here until September 2006.

THE DIAMONDS RESTAURANT AND CABINS

JUNCTION 50·66·100   VILLA RIDGE, MO

A fire so intense that it shut down Route 66 destroyed the restaurant in 1948. A beautiful new streamline moderne fireproof building opened in 1950. The Mission Bell Motel on the north side was expanded to 25 units. Always a promoter, Eckelcamp painted the name on the roof to advertise to aircraft and their passengers.

The third incarnation of the Diamonds stood across from the Gardenway. In 1967, Louis Eckelcamp built a new restaurant and 162-unit motel at the new Interstate 44 interchange with Missouri 100, on the former site of the Mabel Miles Modern Motel. The fast-food joints put it out of business, and the restaurant was torn down in 2007.

This card for the Villa Courts points out that is was two miles west of the Diamonds. Many of the roadside businesses along here touted their proximity to the landmark. The big sign reads "U-Can-Eat Here" while two more boast "We Fix Flats." The place also sold fireworks and Conoco gasoline.

Sunset Motel

U. S. HIGHWAYS 66 AND 50

38 MILES WEST OF ST. LOUIS, MO.

The Sunset Motel was built in the 1940s and is notable for its buff bricks and beautiful sign. The motel advertised "12 units — 12 baths and family suite — beautiful carpets — Panel Ray heat — Beautyrest mattresses — free air conditioned — quiet — free T.V." The Sunset is still in operation today and was recently remodeled.

AMERICAN INN HIGHWAY 50 AND 66, VILLA RIDGE, MO.

Now the Love and Learn Child Care Center, the American Inn was built about 1930 and consisted of two buildings. The stone building on the left served as the garage and gas station. The bottom floor of the log cabin was a restaurant known for Sunday chicken dinners. The upstairs was a residence.

The Hilltop Cafe was operated by Max and Laverta Pracht near Hilltop Road where Route 66 descends into Bourbeuse River Valley. There were no tables, just 23 stools at the counter. A T-bone steak dinner for $1.65 was the most expensive item on the menu. The Hilltop closed afer the arrival of I-44 and no longer stands.

"A better court for better people," the Pin-Oak motel was "clean with 28 ultra modern units." The card touts the cabins with "Stewart-Warner Saf-Aire Heaters." The cabins each had attached carports, which were later enclosed. The pretty little court was converted into storage units, which have since been abandoned and ransacked.

Eastbound on 66 near U.S. 50, billboards touting the Red Cedar Inn, the Park Plaza Courts, the Lennox and Mayfair Hotels, and the Diamonds greeted travelers. Lady Bird Johnson's Highway Beautification Act of 1965 put restrictions on the use of billboards, harming small businesses bypassed by the interstates. The big companies found ways around the law, and today the billboards on Interstate 44 are much larger and more numerous. (Courtesy of the National Archives.)

"THE TWIN BRIDGES"
HWY 66 OVER BOURBEUSE RIVER
NEAR UNION, MO.
S-208

Just before reaching the Bourbeuse River, Highway 66 split into dual lanes, then crossed on the landmark Twin Bridges. Today the Interstate 44 outer road crosses where the bridge on the north side was, and locals still call it the Twin Bridges. The name of the river is pronounced "burr-buss." It is derived from French, meaning "muddy."

BUD & ROY'S PLACE
ON HI-WAY 66
6 miles East of St Clair, Mo.

Bud and Roy's was also known as the Oak Grove Cafe. It was originally the 41 Mile Post, a tavern, store, and cabins built in the 1930s. When the route was known as the Old Wire Road, it was common for businesses to be named for the distance to St. Louis. The foundation for the pumps remains, along with four cabins converted to homes.

Hall's Place four miles east of St. Clair was built about 1930. This view shows Frank Hall's two-story home at the center. Hall had 17 stills cranking out bootleg whiskey to sell here. The station was torn down to make room for the Interstate 44 service road. The remainder was later known as the Hilltop Cafe. The house still stands.

This view of the Four Seasons Cabins and Café dates from September 1961. Tom Hoff built the Four Seasons in 1927, the first local business to open on the newly paved Route 66. The Four Seasons included a tavern, a store, and a gas station. The building still stands and is a private residence. (Courtesy of the St. Clair Historical Museum.)

PERCY'S MOTOR CO.--ST. CLAIR, MO.--PHONE 43---Used Cars & Parts
FERGUSON TRACTORS & IMPLEMENTS

Percy Dickinson ran Percy's Motor Company, a used car and farm implement dealership at the east end of St. Clair. It looks like there was quite a selection of old vehicles for parts in back. The building is still recognizable. It now houses the Pierce Window and Door Company at 1236 North Commercial Street. (Courtesy of the St. Clair Historical Museum.)

This card shows the new four-lane at the interchange with Missouri 47. Signs directed motorists "to St. Clair—go underneath bridge and make two right turns." The town was originally known as Traveler's Repose until residents got tired of being mistaken for a cemetery. It was renamed for a resident Frisco Railroad civil engineer in 1859.

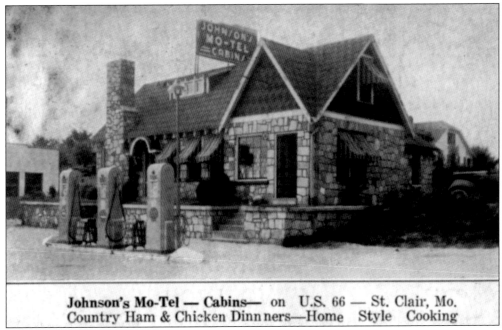

Johnson's Mo-Tel — Cabins— on U.S. 66 — St. Clair, Mo.
Country Ham & Chicken Dinnners—Home Style Cooking

Charlie and Liza Johnson built the Johnson's Mo-Tel and Cabins about 1940. They had three sons in the Army Air Corps, so the place was known to give extra special care to servicemen. The card notes they specialized in country ham and chicken "dinnners." A real estate office occupies the building today.

The Hi Spot Inn was the first business to open on the new U.S. 66 that bypassed the main business district in 1927. Route 66 originally followed the path of the Old Springfield Road, Missouri 14, through town. The business was owned by a Mr. Kemper, whose family lived in the back. Apartments were later built on the site. (Courtesy of the St. Clair Historical Museum.)

Reed's Service Station was located at the corner of Main and Commercial Streets. The site was later occupied by the Keith Wilson Insurance Company. The station sold Skelly gasoline with K-27 for "a cleaner motor and faster start." It also offered "liquor, clean cabins and restrooms." (Courtesy of the St. Clair Historical Museum.)

The Lewis Cafe at 145 South Main Street is still the place to be if one is hungry in St. Clair. The place has been serving up home-cooked meals since 1938. This early-1960s card notes that it specialized in steaks, chicken, shrimp, and homemade pies and "popular prices prevail."

The Schloss Hotel is now the site of the American Legion post at the intersection of Route 66 (Missouri 47) and Missouri 30. It offered hot biscuits and nut waffles, along with "Chicken and Steak Dinners and Short Orders, Served at Any Hour." The hotel promised "Reasonable Rates" and a "Homelike Environment."

Harty's Dine-O-Tel at Route 66 and Missouri 30 had a tavern and diner on the ground floor and rooms upstairs. It was built for Roger Harty around 1937. The Dine-O-Tel promised "Deluxe Dining Service" and was "the Home of Chicken in the Hay." The building operated for a time as the Surf Lounge. Extensively remodeled, it is now a beauty salon.

The same family has operated Ritter and Sons since 1931. This two-story addition was built in 1947. Arthur B. Ritter and his sons Jerome and Danny added a playground and park for their customers. It included a shuffleboard court, a merry-go-round, and a picnic area. The building still looks much the same today. (Courtesy of the St. Clair Historical Museum.)

The St. Clair Motel was built in the early 1940s and is still standing. Postcards show it has been operated at various times by Mr. and Mrs. Pete Krifka, Fred and Mary Leen, Faye Hermling, and Walter and Kitty Crumbacker. The Krifkas hoped their card carried "good news of a pleasant and restful pause in a happy journey."

Some of the local residents say the New England Pantry was a "ritzy place." The restaurant started out as a private residence. It is still there today and once again is a private home. One postcard says the restaurant was 47 miles west of St. Louis, while another puts it 50 miles west of the city.

The Skylark Motel was built about 1955 by Charlie Johnson and his son Robert Charles Johnson on the new highway west of town. They formerly ran the Johnson's Mo-Tel (also known for a time as Art's) in St. Clair. Note the distinctive pillar with glass block insets on the front of the building, which is now the VFW hall.

Arch Bart opened his service station west of St. Clair in the late 1920s. It developed into Scully's Sunset Inn. Scully was once a chef at the famous Busch's Grove Restaurant in St. Louis. The restaurant moved to the north outer road in 1952. One day it just closed, and the tables were left set for years. Agape House now occupies the building.

Paul Jacob Woodcock, a Nazarene minister, got into the rock business when he was paid in blue tiff for helping a miner. The miner said the rare rock would sell if Woodcock put it in front of his home. His wife, Lola May, began making rock curios by the thousands. This view shows the first incarnation of the business.

OZARK ROCK CURIOS   ST. CLAIR, MO.

The original location continued to grow, and Paul Jacob Woodcock even added gas pumps. When the four-lane was constructed in 1948, Ozark Rock Curios moved to the outer road. In 1963, Woodcock went west to minister to the Navajo. The business closed in 1977. Only the house Woodcock built at the second location still stands.

This view shows one of the displays at Ozark Rock Curios. At one time, there were 10 stands, the first starting off with rocks selling for 10¢. As tourists moved down the line, the prices got higher. The last one held stones that could cost hundreds of dollars. Paul Jacob Woodcock mined stalactites from smaller caves to sell to Meramec Caverns. (Courtesy of the St. Clair Historical Museum.)

HILLIARD'S ROCK VILLAGE — Highway 66 — St. Clair, Mo.

Leslie and Margie Hilliard ran the Hilliard Restaurant and Motel five miles west of St. Clair. Margie's fried chicken was famous. There was no counter, just a few tables. That was because Margie's doll collection took up most of the space. She began selling dolls along with rock curios outside.

Margie Hilliard's dolls were high quality, some with price tags to match. The construction of Interstate 44 forced customers to backtrack a long way on the service road to reach the business, but it survived. Leslie died in 1976, and Margie passed away in 1988. Her collection was sold at auction, and the business was torn down.

The Alamo Café was a later incarnation of Leroney's, near Route 66 and St. Louis Inn Road. Built in 1930, it was originally known as Bracket's Place. Ed Leroney expanded it to include a service station, dance hall, and six cabins. It burned down in the late 1940s. The Alamo Café itself burned down in 1952.

The Log Cabin Inn was located five miles west of St. Clair across the road from the Ozark Tourist Court. The sign promised "Good Eats." The place was "Open Nights" and reportedly offered a good selection of souvenirs. One of the guest cabins is visible on the left. It was torn down for the new four-lane Route 66/ Interstate 44.

The Ozark Tourist Court was built about 1930 and is shown here in 1956. The complex was owned by a fellow with the last name of Duke, a retired St. Louis police officer. Duke was the local justice of the peace. With his two deputies, he created a speed trap and his own little kangaroo court to collect the fines.

A fellow known as "Indian Joe" ran the Tepee souvenir stand west of the Ozark Tourist Court. He lived in the back, sold pottery, and advertised "cards and letters mailed here." The place caught fire in the late 1930s, and Indian Joe jumped down the cistern to escape the flames. He escaped the fire but drowned in the cistern.

This was the original café of the Ozark Tourist Court, before it was enlarged in 1950. The complex included a service station, cabins, and a café. It also offered souvenirs and pottery. Only a small portion still stands on the North Service Road. It is much harder to spot since the distinctive sign with its deer logo was removed.

16 All Approved AAA Modern Cabins 24 Hr. Cafe

BENSON'S TOURIST CITY

7 Miles West of St. Clair, Mo. U. S. Hiway 66

"Clean, Respectable, Your Home Away From Home" was the motto of Benson's Tourist City. Mr. and Mrs. Lewis J. Benson offered 16 AAA-approved cabins. Mr. and Mrs. R. E. McGinnis later operated it as the McGinnis Sho-Me Courts, and it was also known as the Del-Crest. Part of the complex still stands.

Jesse and Louise Renshaw were operating the Trade Winds Motel, six miles west of St. Clair, when this view was made. The place had a nice swimming pool, featured television and air-conditioning, and was "open year round." A sign still stands, but most of the complex burned down.

Silver Star Court was famous for putting a twist on the venerable roadside snake pit. It was the home of "the Snake Man." He lived in a hole for 30 days at a time with his slithery friends. Visitors paid a quarter to watch through a glass cover, often seeing him pick up rattlers and squirt venom on the glass. The court was torn down in the 1970s.

The Motel Meramec at Lollar Branch Road was a home converted into a motel advertised as "clean modern cabins and rooms with a dining room in connection, strictly home cooking." Originally the building faced the railroad tracks. When Highway 66 was constructed, it was turned around to face the highway.

SULLIVAN, MO.   **KOVAC'S**   **66**   **44**

WHERE CHICKEN & DUMPLINGS ARE DEE-LICIOUS

The Motel Meramec became Kovac's. The Kafe's chicken and dumplings were "dee-licious," and it was also known for ham and beans. The menu urged visitors to "look over our selection of novelties." The building today is a private residence. This view is from 1964 and for some reason says the location was in Sullivan.

ACACIA SHADY REST COURT . . . U.S. Hwy. 66 . . . Stanton, Missouri

The Acacia Shady Rest Court was a quarter mile east of the turnoff to Meramec Caverns. In 1951, the Shady Rest included a trailer park, "clean, quiet, modern cabins," and a restaurant in connection with "home cooking." The motel at 2665 North Service Road became the Happy Acres Residential Care Center.

STANTON MOTEL
Located on Highway 66 at Stanton, Mo.

The Stanton Motel billed itself as the closest to Meramec Caverns. It also advertised central heat, tubs or showers, low rates, and winter rates. The Stanton Motel is still in business on the north side of Interstate 44, and the original sign is still there. The bright red sign looks like it was recently restored.

Armistead's Supply Store at Stanton was in business for the first few years Route 66 was open. The store not only sold gas and groceries but also housed the post office. The town was originally known as Reedville. It was later named for Peter Stanton, who operated a copper mine and powder mill here in the 1850s. (Courtesy of the St. Clair Historical Museum.)

This view of Stanton was mailed in 1936 and is looking east. Hammer's General Store is on the left. It later became Crawford's Market before being torn down for the Interstate 44 ramps. The building among the trees to the right was Effie and Louis Wurzburger's Place. Wurzburger's was known not only for good food but for gambling too.

This was a typical scene about 1964, as tourists who have turned off Route 66 onto the road to Meramec Caverns wait for a Frisco Railroad train to pass. The old post office is on the left. In its early days, this was reportedly the most robbed post office in Missouri. Crawford's Market is on the right. (Courtesy of the St. Clair Historical Museum.)

The most famous roadside attraction in Missouri was discovered in 1720. Salt Petre Cave provided an important ingredient for gunpowder. Legend says Jesse James hid out here while riding with Quantrill's Guerillas during the Civil War. Locals staged dances in a subterranean ballroom. Lester Dill bought the cave on May 1, 1933.

PARKING INSIDE MERAMEC CAVERNS
STANTON MO. U.S. HY. 66

Lester Dill did not have time to build a parking lot by opening day, so Meramec Caverns became the "World's Only Drive In Cave." About 200 cars could fit inside. Tourists rolled their windows down in the cave and took off in air-conditioned comfort for the first few miles. Dill was a marketing genius and is credited with inventing the bumper sticker.

RAPES IN WINE ROOM 5TH FLOOR MERAMEC CAVERNS
STANTON MO. U.S. HV 66 D 294
L.L.COOK CO MILWAUKEE. WIS.

Meramec Caverns was billed as the world's only five-story cave. Formations included Onyx Mountain, "the world's largest known stalagmite." Lester Dill is in the Wine Room, showing the naturally formed grapes. Other formations were given fanciful names such as Entrance to Paradise, Capitol Dome, and King Solomon's Pillar.

WORLD'S ONLY 5 STORY CAVE

On Highway 66 S.W. of ST. LOUIS

MERAMEC CAVERNS
STANTON MISSOURI

Lester Dill gave the formations names like the Virgin Mary and the Stage Curtain. The tour still ends at the Stage Curtain, where an American flag in colored lights is projected on the formation and a scratchy recording of Kate Smith's "God Bless America" plays. It's American roadside hucksterism at its best.

In the 1930s, Dill saw an advertisement for Lookout Mountain painted on the side of a barn. Soon Meramec Cavern barns appeared all over the Midwest. Dill declared his cave as the "World's First Atomic Refuge." Visitors were even given cards that guaranteed admission if the bombs fell. This photograph was captioned "Frank and Barbara Anne holding Colonel."

In 1942, Lester Dill claimed he found some rusty old relics in the cave that could be traced to Jesse James. In 1949, he claimed to have produced James in person. The media ate up the story when Dill and his son-in-law brought 102-year-old J. Frank Dalton to Stanton and said he was the famous outlaw.

The Cavern City Hideout Motel is still in operation today. Dill opened it as the Cavern City Courts. For a time, it was known as the Ozark Tourist Bureau, handing out information and maps as well as selling souvenirs and gas. The Wall family has operated it since 1956, and this building now serves as the office. (Courtesy of the St. Clair Historical Museum.)

Preston Pryser, a retired corncob pipe salesman from Washington, Missouri, named the Martha Jane Auto Court after his wife. It was one of the first between St. Louis and Springfield with hot and cold water, showers, and toilets in each cottage. The driveway has moved, but the left entrance pillar is still there.

Pryser built a miniature farm out front to attract business. He was also known to lure travelers with a sign that read "Stop—See the Bats—Free!" Hapless travelers would then be shown a few old baseball bats. The house still stands, the yard now filled with plastic deer, turkey, and other animals.

The White Swan Restaurant and Standard service station is shown here about 1940. The White Swan also served as the Sullivan Greyhound bus stop for many years. It later became the White Swan Tavern. The complex was torn down in 1989, and Strasser's Pharmacy occupies this site today.

The Sullmo was a private residence converted to a hotel and cabins by 1935. The card says the Sullmo was "equipped completely with Simmons Beds, double coil springs specially made mattresses." Proprietor Charles Albrecht promised the drinking water was "pure as a lilly." St. Anthony's School was built on the site.

GRANDE COURTS, Sullivan, Mo.

Located on the North Side of Town U. S. Highway 66

The Grande Courts were "the Pride of Sullivan." There were 40 rooms, "strictly modern cottages with free garages," a beautiful courtyard swimming pool, and even an all-night watchman. Later extensively remodeled, it became the 34-unit Hitching Post Motel. The Family Motor Inn occupies the site today.

Snell's Cafe was the home of "Awful good Food." Mr. and Mrs. Fred Snell Sr. served steaks, chicken dinners, and seafood and offered fountain service. It was remodeled into the Hitching Post Restaurant, featuring "Pipin" hot pan biscuits and apple butter. The building is now an antiques mall.

The Sunrise Motel was a "modern motel featuring tile baths, air conditioning, television, and family units." In its later years, the hotel had a very distinctive sign rising high above the north service road. The Sunrise was still standing until the fall of 2007, when it was torn down for an improved Interstate 44 interchange.

SHAMROCK COURT
U. S. Hwy. 66
Sullivan, Missouri

An Italian stonemason named Grandpa Berti built the Shamrock Motel in 1945 for F. E. Dobbs. The motel is actually just across the Crawford County line. Between each opening in the facade is a sunburst in Ozark stone. This card described the Shamrock as "Big, Airy, quiet homelike cabins." This beautiful building still stands.

Five

METRO EAST

Route 66 originally left Edwardsville on Hillsboro Street, Main Street, St. Louis Street, West Street, and St. Louis Road to Chain of Rocks Road. At Mitchell, it turned onto Nameoki Road (Illinois 203) to Granite City. Drivers continued via Madison Avenue, Thirtieth Street, G Street (now Grand), and Eighteenth Street to State Street, then on Broadway through Madison to the McKinley Bridge. The route shifted to the Municipal Bridge (MacArthur) in 1929, over a long list of streets to the bridge at Piggott Avenue in East St. Louis. In 1936, the main route returned to Mitchell again, this time to the Chain of Rocks Bridge. The Municipal Bridge route then became City 66. In 1955, 66 shifted to the new interstate from Worden to U.S. 40 west of Troy. The route across the Chain of Rocks became Bypass 66-40, and City 66 was discontinued. From this time until construction of Interstate 55/70, 66 used Collinsville Road, which became Ninth Street, and State Street (M. L. King) to the bridge. Route 66 moved to the Poplar Street Bridge on November 9, 1967.

Edwardsville was founded in 1816 and is the third-oldest city in the state. The city is named for the first territorial governor, Ninian Edwards. Edwards created Madison County and put the county seat in a town laid out by his friend Thomas Kirkpatrick. Edwardsville celebrates the Mother Road with a Route 66 festival each June.

This view is from 1940, showing the homecoming parade traveling down East Vandalia Street toward Main Street. The Bohm Building is on the left, at that time occupied by a drugstore. Kriege Hardware is visible on the right side of the street, looking much the same as it does today. (Courtesy of the Madison County Historical Society.)

In this view of Main Street and Route 66, arrows point the way for Illinois Route 159 to Wood River and Illinois Route 112 to Bunker Hill, while the sign directs Route 66 to St. Louis straight ahead. The Deep Rock gas station is charging 12¢ per gallon. The brand-new 1940 DeSotos have arrived at the dealership. (Courtesy of the Madison County Historical Society.)

George B. Cathcart's Cafe at 456 East Vandalia Street was "Known from Coast to Coast for Quality Food and Service." There were 21 employees keeping the place open day and night, and Cathcart had a room next door and a bed in back to keep an eye on them. The restaurant could hold 250 people.

The Edwardsville High School building opened in 1925, a year before Route 66 was commissioned. It was designed by M. B. Kane of Edwardsville. Due to a shortage of funds, the gymnasium was not added on until 1928. There were several more additions made to the building over the years. A new high school opened in 1997. (Courtesy of the Madison County Historical Society.)

Orval and Virginia Legate operated Legate's Modern Motel and the Hilltop House Restaurant from 1948 to 1964 at the top of Tanyard Hill. (There once was a tanning yard at the top along what is now Illinois 157.) A couple could stay here for $6 per night, and patrons could catch their own dinner in the motel's three-acre lake.

The Bel-Air west of Illinois 111 opened during the heyday of the drive-in, the 1950s. It could handle 700 cars and was still showing films as late as 1987. Since then, grass has grown up over the lot, and the screen has fallen down. The marquee survives for now, but the area is developing rapidly.

Mid-West Motel, U. S. 66, By Pass U. S. 40
Mitchell, Illinois

The Mid-West Motel stood on Bypass 40-66 (now Chain of Rocks Road) three miles east of the Chain of Rocks Bridge. The "Ultra Modern" motel had electric heat and "U.S. Koylon Foam Mattresses." AAA said it was "a good motel" with "nicely furnished rooms" starting at $6 per night in 1959.

The Luna Cafe is older than Route 66. The Luna also had a gambling operation in the basement, and Al Capone is said to have frequented the joint. Legend says when the red cherry in the glass on the sign was lit, that meant the ladies of the night were working upstairs. The girls are gone, but the Luna is still open.

In 1953, the Corps of Engineers built a canal to carry barge traffic around the treacherous Chain of Rocks on the Mississippi River. The Canal Motel was the last on Bypass 40-66 before the highway crossed the canal and the Chain of Rocks Bridge over the Mississippi. It is still in business today, on what is now Chain of Rocks Road, west of Illinois 3.

These signs greeted travelers headed west as Route 66, now Chain of Rocks Road, approached the Chain of Rocks Canal. The Land of Lincoln Motel sign with its diamond-shaped marquee no longer stands. The Chain of Rocks Motel sign was removed in 2006 when the motel became an Economy Inn.

Frederick and William Niedringhaus opened a new plant to manufacture their Granitware cooking utensils on Six Mile Prairie in 1891. They incorporated Granite City in 1896. In 1896, the business was named the National Enamel and Stamping Company (NESCO). Over 4,000 people worked here in 1910. The NESCO plant closed in 1956 and was mostly destroyed by fire in 2003. (Courtesy of the Madison County Historical Society.)

The Niedringhaus brothers opened a steel mill to supply their plant in 1895. At the beginning of the 20th century, as many as 5,000 European immigrants arrived each year to work at NESCO, Granite City Steel, and the other big plants that followed. National Steel bought Granite City Steel in 1971, and U.S. Steel acquired National in 2003. (Courtesy of the Madison County Historical Society.)

East St. Louis was originally known as Illinoistown. The National Civic League named it an "All-American City" in 1959. But the factories closed, and whites fled to the suburbs. Today most of the buildings in this view are vacant. The 13-story Spivey Building in this view is the tallest in southern Illinois. But the abandoned building is completely decrepit and may be torn down.

BIBLIOGRAPHY

Curtis, C. H. *The Missouri U.S. 66 Tour Book*. Lake St. Louis: Skip Curtis Enterprises, 1994.

Dippell, Jane. "What a Hideout." *Show Me Route 66 Magazine*. Route 66 Association of Missouri, Summer 2007.

Graham, Shellee. *Tales from the Coral Court*. St. Louis: Virginia Publishing, 2000.

Magnan, William B. and Marcella C. *The Streets of St. Louis*. St. Louis: Virginia Press, 1994.

Powell, Jim. "U.S. Highway 66 in Missouri: A Historical Perspective." *Show Me Route 66 Magazine*. Route 66 Association of Missouri, Fall 2001.

Repp, Thomas Arthur. *Route 66: Empires of Amusement*. Lynnwood, WA: Mock Turtle Press, 1999.

Scott, Quinta. *Along Route 66*. Norman: University of Oklahoma Press, 2000.

Snyder, Tom. *Route 66 Travelers Guide and Roadside Companion*. New York: St. Martins Press, 1990, 1995.

Sonderman, Joe. *St. Louis 365*. St. Louis: Stellar Press 2003.

Wallace, Michael. *Route 66: The Mother Road*. New York: St. Martins Press, 1994.

Wickline, David. *Images of 66*. Westerville, OH: Roadhouse 66, 2006.

Writers Program of the Works Progress Administration. *Missouri: A Guide to the Show Me State*. Missouri State Highway Department, 1941.

Discover Thousands of Local History Books
Featuring Millions of Vintage Images

Arcadia Publishing, the leading local history publisher in the United States, is committed to making history accessible and meaningful through publishing books that celebrate and preserve the heritage of America's people and places.

Find more books like this at
www.arcadiapublishing.com

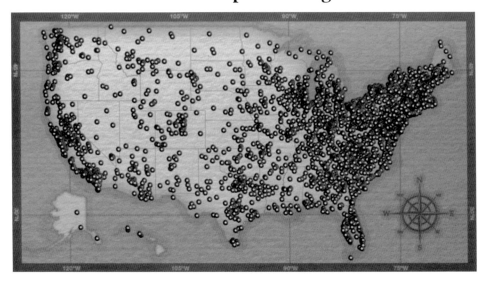

Search for your hometown history, your old stomping grounds, and even your favorite sports team.

Consistent with our mission to preserve history on a local level, this book was printed in South Carolina on American-made paper and manufactured entirely in the United States. Products carrying the accredited Forest Stewardship Council (FSC) label are printed on 100 percent FSC-certified paper.